## PRAISE FOR
### *LOVE IS THE DRUG & OTHER DARK POEMS*

"*Love Is the Drug & Other Dark Poems* is infinitely readable. Next time you need to be consoled or need to be reminded that you're not the only one having troubles with love, I recommend spending a few hours with this slim, many-voiced collection of poetry. It will cure whatever ails you. If I were a doctor, I'd tell you to take two and call me in the morning."

**—Carl Adamshick, author of *Saint Friend***

"Reader beware: These audacious, daring, often heartbreaking poems will shove love, with all its messy, unwieldy glory, in your face. Featuring the work of 33 poets and 8 artists, this astonishing collection explores the underbelly of love from remarkably divergent perspectives. Yet each poet in some way posits the question: How can love survive in today's world, with its high expectations and infinite distractions? 'I walked toward you with a limp/ my left leg forced to carry the weight/ of this *thing* in my chest/ that is supposed to be in love.' (Kelsey Kundera, 'Sunflower Seeds'). These poems, and the edgy art that accompanies them, go a long way toward answering that question."

**—Alexis Rhone Fancher, author of *Junkie Wife***

"Poetry is my first love, and with this spectacular collection, I am reminded why. The aliveness I felt as I read each complex and unique piece in this book had me shaking my fist at the sky with knowing, had me tearing up, had me excited, had me heartbroken, had me undone. That's what a good poem does. A good poem makes you feel all the things in a moment as quick as a breath, yet it remains with you long after you have exhaled. It remains with you in your body. That is what this book does. It lives in your body and I am thrilled to see it out in the world. To call this book good would be simple. This book is the drug, this book is the love, this book is life."

**—Jennifer Pastiloff, author of *On Being Human***

"*Love Is the Drug* is so shimmering and personal. These little moments when we achieve, with the aid of another, some kind of sublime, and time and space sort of dissolve and we're right where it feels we're meant to live—those little moments are quick sparkles, these efforts to pin them down in poetry feel as sweaty and muscular, as desperate and full of passion, as the sex itself. Each one a little flare, a little death, an *I was here*."
—**Michelle Tea, author of *Against Memoir* and *Black Wave***

"It's a strange condition of desire, that it can only be expressed in relation to absence; love lost, love not yet consummated, love unrequited, most articulate in the hand that reaches, and evidenced in these pages in repetitions of *want* and *you*. To *yearn toward* is the potent, aching stuff of poetry, and youth, and melodrama—one must risk a little drama, I believe, to touch the subject of passionate love. It's a difficult task, but as García Lorca wrote, 'To burn with desire and keep quiet about it is the greatest punishment we can bring on ourselves.' Within these pages, that burning speaks. These mouths, in love and out, are articulate wounds, and as these poets have it, the 'wound is nothing without your tongue,' and the lover can only 'lick like flames/ at the edges.' Love, in fact, is a drug—a cocktail really, of noradrenaline, oxytocin, dopamine. In love, we are on drugs, and out of love we crave the next hit. Maybe that's why there's so much sugar in these pages, sweets and syrups employed as metaphor for what the Beloved withholds, the drug to set the lover free. Reader, prick up your ears! A choir of unruly, ardent, and embodied poems is singing."
—**Lisa Wells, author of *The Fix***

"Within this book lives the profound work of pain turned into poetry, and that poetry, into power. These poems hold the best, most beautiful, brutal, sharp, and tender words of these wise and generous writers. My gratitude for their brilliance and generosity is endless. Elixir and companion, keep this book close. Let it leave your side only so that it may be shared with others."
—**Reema Zaman, author of *I Am Yours***

LOVE IS THE DRUG & OTHER DARK POEMS

# LOVE IS THE DRUG & OTHER DARK POEMS

EDITED by JESSIE CARVER & JENNIFER LEWIS

"Maggie" by Bradley Penner and "Love Poem Number Carrot" by Kristina Ten were first published in *sPARKLE & bLINK*; "Notes on Tenderness" by kiki nicole was first published in *Vagabond City Literary Journal*.


ISBN 13: 978-0-9998895-0-3
Library of Congress Control Number: 2018937475
First edition, printed July 2018


Cofounder & editor in chief: Jennifer Lewis
Editor: Jessie Carver
Cover photograph: Lucille Lares-Kiwan
Book design: Brian David Smith
Text set in Mr Eaves Modern & Adobe Garamond Pro


Printed in the United States of America


Made with love

# CONTENTS

## INTRODUCTION

Red Light Lit began in 2013 as a live, curated show in San Francisco featuring poetry, prose, art, and song, and accompanied with a printed literary journal. Over the years and with each new show across the country, we're reminded just how compelling poetry and prose can be when choreographed with live music and photography. In this anthology, we feature the work of 33 writers and 8 artists, each offering a distinctive voice and texture that coalesces into an experience that we view as a natural extension of our shows.

The poems and photographs in these pages speak to each other—some in conversation, some in call and response, some in reflection. The only contributor who hasn't previously been featured in a Red Light Lit event is kiki nicole; when we came across their work, we felt like we found a kindred spirit. In "Notes on Tenderness" they write, "i don't know how to turn the Ugly off." *Love Is the Drug & Other Dark Poems* does not contain sweet, lighthearted verses about romance. Even in "Faith," the most reverent poem of the anthology, Josey Rose Duncan tenderly states, "You are the bacteria to my gutless marine worm." This book is not pretty, yet each poet's honesty is incredibly beautiful.

*Love Is the Drug* attempts to answer questions like: Who do we become when we lose ourselves to lust, when we become dependent on or addicted to the chemistry of another? What happens when we try to pin down the moment when lust turns to love? What happens when we betray someone we love or when we are betrayed?

As the poems exemplify, this type of exploration is inextricable from the body and involves scars, wounds, blood, and teeth. So many teeth. Teeth that mark bodies, that snarl with hunger, that are broken and "scattered...round town like time bombs" (Lara Coley, "Extraction"). But it's not all loneliness, longing, and pain. There are sinkholes of love filled with ardent lines like "You are the light on the nights' black bay water" and "Your voice is a Wagner leitmotif with the current of crimson" from Monique Mero in "Swallow."

Reading these poems side by side feels like a revelation. *Love Is the Drug* exposes the intimate, sometimes disturbing intricacies of navigating love, sex, relationships, and loss in a way that seems new and important. This anthology reveals the emotionally raw spectrum of the human experience that is at once familiar and intriguing, comforting and thrilling, startling and validating. Regardless of personal history, race, gender, sexual orientation, or religion, we share overlapping desires, joys, comforts, pains, and fears.

These poems emerge from diverse communities of writers across the country, many of whom know and inspire each other. And we hope these poems inspire more people to write—and then keep writing!—because communities need new writers just as much as established writers need communities to flourish. As Bradley Penner asserts in "Maggie": "But I've come to write. What's put down is done. Then again, same with love."

Jessie Carver, editor
Portland, Oregon
&
Jennifer Lewis, cofounder & editor in chief
San Francisco, California

**HANNAH BURGOS**

**VALENTINE**
by **CHRISTINE NO**

You called me your:

Oxytocin
Serotonin
Dopamine
Dream girl
Norepinephrine queen

Rapid cycling
Mood shifter
Horse power
Trigger finger
Off road attic
Eroded arc
Mettle
Metal
Heart

## THE END OF OUR CASUAL FUCKING
by **SARAH BETHE NELSON**

Desperate to not lose our last
Tethers to The Cult of Who Knows
(each other) (a dying breed)
Desperate to not show desperation
We tell our secrets
Some we just know,
And that hurts and feels good
So we press on
When one of us is naked
Standing before the other
More naked even than naked
The clothed one cannot help
But reach out to touch,
To soothe, to become naked, too
So much so that our tongues
Melt and we dissolve, depraved
Into our own true natures
This ritual, teeth and blood
We are animals
We mark each other's bodies
We take anything that remains
Of virginity or all the days before
It is as if you are trying to leave
Yourself everywhere
It is as if I am trying to tear out
Your heart and run with it,
Still beating, into the trees.

## SUNDAY MORNING
by **SARAH KOBRINSKY**

We wake up
on dream-spattered sheets,
the ceiling fan re-circulates
last night's love,
dead skin we sloughed off
in our friction
    falls like fairy dust.
Coffee barely covers
the musk we made,
headlines stick to our bodies
and become
    a new story—
*I never want to make*
*this bed again.*
Soon flies will gather
and vultures will near
our beautiful,
    awful mess.
Only then will I strip
these sacred sheets,
trap them in a gilded frame,
and hang them—
    an offering—
above our battered bed.

**TOD BRILLIANT**

## SUPPOSE I ALWAYS KNEW
by **JESSIE CARVER**

Suppose the nibble
of your teeth on my neck,
gentle and ravenous
as the night, was
a warning that I, in willful
unknowing, slipped
between my mattress
and the floor
to be forgotten.

Suppose I loved
you anyway,
allowed your fingers
to chart a path across the
slashes of scars on my skin,
my body an unfamiliar map,
my tangled hair
whispering across
your sandalwood belly.

I suppose I always knew
you belonged in the world
—and not in my empty
arms—but I only wanted
to eat clementines with you and
watch the juice leak down your chin
until our hair turns gray.

## MAGGIE
by **BRADLEY PENNER**

1. Suppose poem a verb: like love: *I poem you, X, I do. I poem you more than X or Y or whathaveyou.* And like love—delicate minutiae, time of attention—poeming, like loving, doesn't care to be found out. Have to. To poem is to love the difficulty of it. The satin strain. Blindfolded, feeling for silk. To find it. Have you?

2. 85th & Broadway. Little brown stone, Central Park. A cut just below your lower lip. Probably the Pop Rocks. The red ones, always. "As if color could be further revealed by *slitting*." The first taste of you was a boiler room. Red is a boiler room. Taking the 1 or 2 into Chelsea for blood oranges.

3. Sherwin-Williams on Broadway, Oakland. You choose Pompeii Blue. I, Meltwater. Most of the kitchen is an afternoon. An after-the-fact. As if pastels resolve rich with the sun. We resolve in swatches of Bluejay. That tweedy bird.

4. This poem isn't about you.

5. Now, suppose *poem as fuck*. The act of. Holes. Streams. Knee. Neck. Dimples of spine. Never does this *poem* mean *forever*. To *fuck* as *poem* is moment. As fleeting as coming. But I've come to write. What's put down is done. Then again, same with love.

6. But back to this blue jay, the one outside my kitchen window. Always pining over what makes another nest. What the other takes. Poems, maybe. Whatever it is, it's always taking. As if to say *Do you see me for all my blue? Do you know why I ruffle this crown?* And the mourning dove says nothing, coos slight in a yellow dusk of window.

7. I used to write poems for you. With you. Now, I just fuck.

8. In the first essay of *Genealogy of Morals*, Nietzsche claims the lamb cannot separate "strength from expressions of strength," that lamb holds the bird of prey "*accountable* for being a bird of prey." What's put down is done. The deed done, the deed being everything. *The doer*: "merely a fiction added to the deed."

9. *The doer* is this poem. Like Nietzsche's flash of lightning, it's the deed of the deed. You see, you love, you fuck, you poem, but it's in lieu of *action*. Action which brought the seeing, loving, fucking, *poem*. Metaphor reacting in metaphor. The act of. But what does Nietzsche know, anyway? Nietzsche never fucked a day in his life. Loved, yes. Too much, even. But that's not the kind of love I'm talking about.

10. *To poem*, then (I guess), is *to will*. The blue jay in meltwater. Meals in the kitchen. To love the fucking. The fucking being *poem*. The peeled blood orange of a subway. To breathe & mirror the verb of it.

## ELEVATOR PITCH
by **HOLLIE HARDY**

What I want to say is
take me home

To ripen and mottle
in the dim light of candles
to open small mouths
and lick like flames
at the edges of you

From the window of your glass elevator
you flutter like a moth
the city pours its artificial stars
across the silent nightscape
dreaming of cages

I want to say
pack your suitcase, gather your ghosts
let's live in the ocean like salt
let's build a tree house of wind and sand
where we can sleep forever in a tangle of limbs

Still we wear our chains
rusting like fear
of a future hole in a future
pocket
counting our seatbelts
counting the rain

I open my mouth to tell you
how hunger binds us together
how the tether of night unties the moon
I open my mouth
but a wren flies out

What I wanted to say was
take me home

**ANTICIPATION**
by **KIMBERLY REYES**

Even love
        love
                lust
        love
love

in the moment

like static
like worry
like doubt
like masturbation
wine on the couch

feels like film and plastic
feels like reel and repetition

feels unreal


      when it arrives

checking your reflection in his eyes.

## NEIGHBOR
by **LISA ALDEN**

Thin plastic sheath over the free Sunday paper and because
it's yours I think of condoms, spent ones dumped in the toilet
then tossed in the trash atop the tissues and floss. I pick up
the paper and push it through your mail slot. This is not a metaphor,

I'm just telling you what happened. I didn't want anyone to know
you're out of town. That was neighborly, wasn't it? When you
think of me, think of your backyard, the plants growing across
the path, the spiders and bees taking over while I lie

unworried by your distance or the rays burning more than tanning
my backside. That was Friday. Yesterday the fog came and stayed.
I ate one blueberry pie and one little quiche. Already I'm losing
my bikini form, wrapping myself in sweets. And when you return

today and find your paper, you don't call to see where
I've gone. Unshowered you come unannounced to my door
under the pretense of gratitude. You look worse than obese,
thin form left by the sucking of wedlock, morbid, ready

to sweat your life back from the precipice. Like this we get to it,
set to making our bodies into summertime foods, jicama, mango,
papaya, the wet arcs of sex, the shapes we prefer
no matter the weather. I adore you like this, past the point

of caring where your hair falls, how the scar on your belly
changes when you don't hold it in. Who's to blame when love,
full-blown, arrives where we swore the almosts of chemistry
and ache would reign? I'm quiet. All is quiet. There's

the way you sounded that first night,
stories that went on so long I forgot what happened
at the beginning, and the way I think of you. Yes,
your cock specifically. The weight of it before, force

of it rising, solid creature so quickly finding a home,
pushing at the mail slot of my cervix asking if our children
may begin. When you say please this way, yes, please.
There is no answer but yes, even questions

not yet asked. Yes, I like it. Yes, I know. There's a little more
pie in the kitchen, yes. Your eyes are exactly the right shade
for this next move. Yes, yes, yes. I hate it when we say
probable things during sex. I thought about you, yes. Yes.

## EXTRACTION
### by **LARA COLEY**

Remember that time you did that thing that
made me love you even more and when I
leaned in to breathe the belief you ripped my
teeth out from my expectant lips and
scattered them round town like time bombs
so that as long as I lived here I could walk
down any street and be shattered by a part of
my own brokenness?

I do.

## EROS
by **LARA COLEY**

I string hearts
like pearls,
wear them cynically
to weddings.
I wash myself
with soft, sweaty nights,
make bodies my bathtubs,
tongues and fingertips
scrub my skin,
grant salvation
in hot licks of saliva.
I dress in silks and dew
but catch myself
in bar mirrors
wearing nothing
but want.

**AUBREY JANELLE**

## LOVE POEM NUMBER CARROT
by **KRISTINA TEN**

I'm thinking of a time you made Uzbek plov with your grandfather, who called it a man's dish because it demanded physical strength.

The carving of the fatty lamb, the lifting of the thick-bottomed stockpot, the tearless chopping of onions in the corner.

Never mind the dried apricot that made it sweet. Never mind that he had previously taught you to marinate swordfish in vodka to kill the smell. *Napishitye.*

Never mind the force it takes to suck when you say SUCK, *e proglotitye,* on a clove of cooked garlic. Served on the side, the traditional way, with long, curly ribbons of chapped skin peeled from a carrot.

*Lyubov morkov.* Unwrap me like a gift, I said. I said, Unwrap me like a gift.

I'm thinking of a time we played drunken pond hockey, the recipe for which is a fifth of Rumple Minze, two sticks, and a death wish. Steal your dog's favorite tennis ball, look nosebleed beautiful. Go for the hat trick.

I'm thinking of a town whose main streets are called Church and Water, as if fundamentals run parallel, as if one is as essential as the other. *Pozhaluista.*

I'm thinking of a time my mother said, Perhaps the greatest injustice of all is that the average person gets fewer than 80 Christmases.

*Ya ne panimayu vas.* I'm thinking of another time when she said, The good life is expensive but it's the only one I want.

You love someone honey-thick and amber-hard. You love someone so much and he treats you like furniture.

So you learn to be heartbroken but functional. You become fluent in Inoffensive Wallpaper. *Gavoritye gromche.*

I'm thinking of a time you nicknamed me Kid. Red. Hon. I'm thinking of a time I bequeathed you Lord of Monosyllabic Everything. You responded, Contingency Plan.

I'm thinking of a time you called me a taxicab.

Not called me a taxicab but called me Taxicab.

Meaning you could take me any time you wanted but you never knew what it would cost you.

I'm thinking of a time you woke up naturally, without alarm clocks or coffee. Warm and buzzing. It was all hummingbird *voda.* I'm thinking about our love like a garden-path sentence.

The sour drink from the ocean. The old man the boat. This is where the vegetable finds the root

of the problem: I try to breathe through it like the hiccups but it won't go away. Like the hiccups. *Ikoty napalye no bednevo Fedoti.*

What's Portuguese for I like the way your features
are assembled on your face? What's Romanian for
important and funny and helpful and seemingly rich?
What's romance language for

Sweater weather
Harvest
Bravest
Book smart
Rhubarb
Orange you glad
Kitchen
Fondly
The way I feel at 3 p.m. on a Sunday
Missing plov and promises, *obeshchaniye*
And other things only you can make.

**THINGS NOT ALLOWED IN MY BED**
by **ALLYSON DARLING**

hairy ex-boyfriends
peeled garlic and small chickens
breasts that are not mine

**THINGS DATING BRINGS**
by **ALLYSON DARLING**

an upset bedroom
condom in grandma's teacup
a dirty duvet

**TREVER HADLEY**

## CAN I STILL BE A FEMINIST
by **TARA ROSE**

if I hate my period
if I'm a slut
if I like getting hit during sex
if I think I should shave my pits and legs and cunt
If I still don't bother anyway
if I like one night stands
if I'd like to put them on film
if I go to Take Back the Night just to see the person I want to fuck
if I love a man
if I love a man who hates
if I cry to get what I want
if I've cheated
if I've cheated with a man
if I liked it
if I don't think it counts when it's with a woman
if I know it counts anyway
if I'm like Emily Dickinson
if I wanna be Anne Sexton
if I think euphoria periods are conspiracy
if I cringe at orgasming during birth
if I want to sell my underwear on eBay
if I think adoption is the new home birth
if I want to learn to cook a man his dinner
if I don't want to be mysterious
if I want to be worshipped like a Manic Pixie Dream Girl
if I laugh at a cheater's dick getting chopped off
if I don't know enough about circumcision
if I don't think the media is responsible for my low self-esteem
if I still fucking hate them anyway
if I'm just a person, not a woman
if I don't want it all, I just want enough.

## NOTES ON TENDERNESS
### by **KIKI NICOLE**

i.

& i once knew a Truth
i swallowed it whole after we fucked
how it crept thru on the down low,
real slick,
thick & heavy & embarrassing.
love looked at me & exhaled
gushed a song out of their mouth all
"didn't u like it?"
i wanted to say it was all i had to live on.
instead i lingered in the air above their bosom,
said "i have already learned u by heart."
there, i cut a hole so it can breathe,
dabbed perfume before it had even scabbed over.
i tell them i don't not know how to turn the Ugly off.

we paint it gold anyway.


ii.

this open//
stays parched// turns all the water red
we both know something has died in here// so as not to be forgotten
we write an entire history out in sweat//
u kno// the kind that seeps thru your palms on the side of my face//
i arch my back toward your riot//
lick it up like milk// & salivate over my own body


iii.

we keep the lights on

## BEFORE WILD MAGIC
## by SARAH BETHE NELSON

You crawl out of the ocean
Light lifts from my body

You place a magnet in my mouth
Swallow, you say, unbuttoning

Inside of your chest glints
With all your metal pieces

I think of you rusting
Your hair like weeds

I slip off the fire opal
And dress my wound

One day I will forget to want you
It will be morning
    or afternoon
Or I will be inside and not know
    the time of day.

To rid myself of you I shun comfort,
heat, and softness, intoxication and cover

See, you hide in every pleasure
A shadow on my breast

You pull at me, I find you singing in my ears
Smeared across my lips in the middle of the day

I take away the daily rituals
The rewards and payments

(A withdrawn spell, an empty expanse
How expensive you are)

The metal hums, the magnet purrs
I curl toward you. You are too rich

I cough and cough, choking
On blood and pure light

All silence today
Quiet the past ten nights

Prisms on the page disconnect
Like lone links from a chain

Your child, your lover
Your other lovers, these

We nimbly write around
Goodnight, tin man.

I watch until we become shapes of shadows
Pieces of light collapsing into essence

Home from the hunt, head bowed
Gold on shoulders, beaming between legs

I spit out the magnet you laid on my tongue
Here I am, in strange light, without you

Where I was in the beginning,
    before wild magic
    before wild darkness
    before you arrived.

## SWALLOW
by **MONIQUE MERO**

a shape
Your face
enters   the fusiform gyrus   goes to the angular gyrus   inside the parietal lobes
where complex colors are configured
in the insula forms feelings
feverish I want to fuck you feelings
in luminous lavender halos.

the insula (the island of sensations)
contained in the cortex
is an intellectual touch map.
      We feel from the inside.
See, the insula processes internal feelings—
if I walk toward you     my heart begins to boil to a beat    that sends a stream of
dreams that beam bright in the brain       and bring me a flutter of shame.
and if there are stares between you and me   the heart beats fast   the lungs struggle
for and I find a pleasure in panic.
My brain loses oxygen and then I'm simply serotonin.
      Sometimes I wonder if I suffer from solipsism.
are you a projection
a project
or a project projection of me?
      I may suffer from narcissism

Where in the attic of my mind do you exist?
I would lock myself up there like a Willa Cather character
alone with a dressmaker's mannequin
breathing in the corner
coming undone without the assistance of a seamstress

You are like a phantom limb
I place a mirror opposite the remaining whole
which tickles the mind to believe you are there.
I stretch it          watch it wave
take out the pain
and having it gone makes me feel lonely
so I punch at the whole in the mirror until the image becomes distorted again
the phantom returns and I like it that way

with you comes a kaleidoscope of colors
Your voice is a Wagner leitmotif with the current of crimson
Your facial expressions are as colorful      confusing      and connected to time
as Kandinsky

You are the light on the nights' black bay water
I never know how deep it is
The fear of not knowing hits my amygdala
and makes me want to jump in          and swallow.

**FLIGHT**
by **FISAYO ADEYEYE**


1.


love song with wires. love song with blades
in the teeth. another second, and you have

mirror hands, a God-shaped hole like a cup
scooped out of the hot water. bruised angel

hidden in the closet: Bethlehem or Cape
Town slopes in the morning mist



2.


i molt in the shower. he pulls the feathers
from my pelvis with his teeth. i have never

known a gentler type to be waiting
at the top of a bridge, i am kissing him

under the green water. i am a sheet
wrapped up inside another sheet.

wet fruit stems under our tongues,
he sticks his fingers all the way in.

opens me like a mango

**ANTHONY J. HALL**

**MEAL**
by **BARUCH PORRAS-HERNANDEZ**

oh    we've met before    not in a dream    in a cave
where I ate your flesh    after a long hunt through
a thick forest    oh    we were men    two men
that made love in this cave    but then a blade
was punched into meat
I saw you again    black woods at night
you lit the way    with the fireflies shaking
where your eyes used to be    I followed you till the end

then we met again
on a beach    I was silent, for two green butterflies
kissed daintily    on my tongue    you took my hand
I walked    my mouth wide open

    two men
    we were always two men
    making love at the beginning
    always two men making love
    nothing is new but our skin

    two men chasing    each other through    trees
    walking into caves    seeing ourselves frozen
    in an embrace    seeing ourselves
    painted on ancient cave walls

    we have always been two men
    tearing each other apart
    we have always been
    wrestling on the raw earth
       two snakes
          trying to be kind to each other

love is a fist     wet     in the     throat
an apple     placed there     by a God that
kills you and brings you back to life

beds are invented
          we hide knives underneath them
lie down     play dead     rocked
by the soft back and forth     of blood

cities are built
          then get infested with crying men
two of them weeping
          at every table          in every bar

at one bar
          I sit alone          waiting

you approach me from     behind
     run your nails across     my scalp

let them dig in     the blood
     you take it to your lips

               make sure it tastes the same
                         as it always has

     I unbutton my     shirt
Stare into your eyes

     *Punch me with your blade*
               *eat my flesh.*

## FINITE IS NOT A METAPHOR FOR FIRE
by **HOLLIE HARDY**

something dark and new
growls or purrs
inside the night circus
where my heart flutters
like a spectacle
in its little cage

the lion, the whip, and

the taste of you lingers
like a season
nicotine and leather
those hands

I've been drinking about my feelings again
here in the forest of us
where everything is newly planted

are we rocks or air?

a flash of teeth
as the tide of you rolls out
light shines through the doorway
like a message from home
like an autumn sun slipping into afternoon

here is a lesson about truth
sculpted of bricks and glass
here is another Manhattan

I am trying to be taller again
and you are teaching me to wait
this cherry is not a metaphor
for loss

the way blood prefers to be inside the body
but rushes away at every opening
a kind of defeat by escaping
this fear of silence which binds the city

I want to see the stars again
I want to walk with you in the rain
I wake up with my hands
folded over my chest like a coffin
sometimes you're here
nestled in the small of my back
and sometimes you're gone

## NONETS FOR OLIVER
by **FISAYO ADEYEYE**

it rains and we dip under plastic
overhangs. streetlights pouring in,
purple and red. he looks like
a saint, his smile as sharp
as a switchblade. clasped
at the lips, he
seems almost
a dead
thing

              i wonder if "magic" is just one's
            fruitless attempt in solving some
               unknown in a person: the
                   metal pan with silver
                    fish caught inside, pushed
                      far under the
                       oak bed, to
                        make him
                          love

every morning opening like this,
south: the wet ring the tea leaves on
the table. the trucks rolling
by his house, across the
road, unfolding like
a dry napkin
over his
red, hot
chest

              that night, touching his body until
               it broke, like Christ's body on the
                cross, like Christ's body in my
                  mouth, flimsy as paper,
                   moistened like wafers.
                    scraps collecting
                      on a black
                      boy's wet
                       beak

## FRONT ROW TAKE ONE PASS IT BACK
by **KRISTINA TEN**

*(read in two voices)*

Front row. Take one. Pass it back.

Front row. Take one. Pass it back.

Front row. Take one. Pass it back.

Front row. Take one. Pass it back.

| | |
|---|---|
| Front row. Take one. Pass it back. | This body is not your moon. |
| Front row. Take one. Pass it back. | This body is not your tree ornament, missed appointment. |
| Front row. Take one. Pass it back. | |
| Front row. Take one. Pass it back. | This body is not your harpoon. |
| Front row. Take one. Pass it back. | This body is not your stock photography. |
| Front row. Take one. Pass it back. | |
| Front row. Take one. Pass it back. | This body is not your duck embryos, boiled and eaten in the shell with hot sauce and vinegar. |
| Front row. Take one. Pass it back. | |
| Front row. Take one. Pass it back. | This body is not your dressmaker. |
| Front row. Take one. Pass it back. | This body is not your folding couch, not your couch unfolding. |

Front row. Take one. Pass it back.     This body is not your undecorated cake.

Front row. Take one. Pass it back.     This body is not your armrest,
                                        not your olive oil.

Front row. Take one. Pass it back.     This body is not your cloud
                                        swollen with storm.

Front row. Take one. Pass it back.     This body is soft soft soft soft soft soft,
                                        not your goat cheese.

Front row. Take one. Pass it back.     This body is not your venom.

Front row. Take one. Pass it back.

Front row. Take one. Pass it back.     This body is not holding its arms
                                        away from its sides for the picture.

Front row. Take one. Pass it back.     This body is not your moon.

Front row. Take one. Pass it back.     This body is not your fat peach,
                                        infection.

Front row. Take one. Pass it back.     This body is not your folk medicine.

Front row. Take one. Pass it back.

Front row. Take one. Pass it back.     This body is not your emergency room,
                                        so white I feel it must be cleaned
                                        every minute, like the bridge painters
                                        who take shifts painting the bridge so
                                        it is never not being painted.

Front row. Take one. Pass it back.     This body is not your soundproofing.

Front row. Take one. Pass it back.     This body is not your bamboo steamer.

Front row. Take one. Pass it back.        This body is not the white bits in your salami.

Front row. Take one. Pass it back.        This body has no balconies.

Front row. Take one. Pass it back.        This body is not sitting with its feet on tippy toes to keep its thighs from spreading wide against the chair.

Front row. Take one. Pass it back.

Front row. Take one. Pass it back.        This body is not your ramekin.

Front row. Take one. Pass it back.

Front row. Take one. Pass it back.        This body is not your flacon.

Front row. Take one. Pass it back.

Front row. Take one. Pass it back.        This body is not your extra side of sweet pickled ginger.

**TOD BRILLIANT**

**IMMUNITY**
by **JESSIE CARVER**

The most honest love
letter I ever received said:
> *I love you but I will betray you.*
> *I betray you because I love you.*
> *I will love you because I betray you.*

I'm still learning the difference between
these acts and delight in the way
my skin weeps with each fresh
tattoo, the corporeal release
following exquisite pain.

At home, the quiet is a
distillation of words
too dangerous to say aloud.

I have a complicated
relationship with trains
and visit airports to cry in
a place I'm not alone,
with passersby too hurried
to register my grief.

I wish I could believe in a god
but trees are more reliable, how
they erupt into furious blossoms
in May, and discard their leaves
without ceremony in November.
They are immune to love
and betrayal, both.

## FOUR
by **DEVIN COPELAND**

It's never enough just to say everything hurts
They won't let you say that
They'll ask which parts
Why
How can we help you
What do you need to solve this problem
Would you like me to find you a therapist
Have you tried meditating
Why don't you come over for dinner tonight
I think you're drinking too much
Try getting into a routine
What do you need
Stay with us
Get up with the sun
You'll feel better
We could go for a hike next weekend!
Fresh air is the cure
You should meet my nephew
Try this fruit
Are you taking vitamins?
You'll be ok


They won't let you just say, no
No
Everything hurts
And it always will

What he did to me
What he didn't do with me
What I did to him
What I didn't do with him
What I let myself do with the other
What I didn't let myself do to the other
What he didn't do to me


What he did do
What he did with her
What she didn't do to him
What she did do
What I did to her
What she wants to do to me
What he wants from me
What he wants to do to the other
What it would do to me
What I did to me
What I didn't let myself be

## NAME YOUR SELF NEW WORLD
by **TOMAS MONIZ**

if only discovery occurred after consent    i would stake &
claim what is found in the way you give thanks    or the way
you resist    i'd seek approval to traverse the soft mounds of
the hurt you carry    proof that everything has an apex    a
beginning & an ending    i'd quarry & excavate places long
ignored as invaluable    your laugh    the back of your knee
the taut muscles above your buttocks    such precious material
if only we could play pillage    if only we could mark x on the
spots we desire return    if only we could caution each other
about the edges    the places where monsters be    if only
we could undo first contact    but we are not unwise    we
understand truth    refuse the willful ignorance so often pedaled
as nostalgia    so lover name your self new world & we can
reenact what collaboration might have looked like

## WHAT WILL SAVE US ALL
by **TOMAS MONIZ**

desire    never satiated & always resurrected    is the true
god    it propels the body to redemption    offers itself up    as
promise & pleasure    as gift & grail    but it's never the actual
thing    the quiet morning coffee    the slap & the choke    the
pizza slice at 11:30 at night    it's impetus    it's forgiveness
it's acquiescence    it's absolution    desire prompts craft    the
creation & the revision    the process of becoming whole    a
new thing    desire's the rediscovery    the repetitive act made
original    familiarity as renewal    it's your mother's frijoles
when you return home    it's finding satisfaction in fucking for
the 737th time    it's knowing the tomorrow might suck but the
bourbon tastes good now    it's a faith in healing    despite the
risks of living    of survival    it's knowing that to want is to be
alive    because the wanting itself is what will save us all

**FEMINIST?**
by **AMBER FLAME**

I fell in love on the way to work today
It was just one of those things
She stepped out in front of me
Head held high
Braids twisted higher
And brown skin glistening
And she dressed like a girl
But walked like a dude
You know, shoulders first
Strong long fingers casually clinging to coffee cup


I wanted to say girl
I wanna stir my coffee into your cream, girl
I wanted to say girl
Let me bury my nose in the nappy edges of your hair, girl
I wanted to say girl
Let me lick salt sticky sweet from your earlobe, girl
I wanted to say girl
Let me put my ice cream cone into your dipping chocolate, girl


But just like that
She stepped inside
Wherever she was going
And I found myself wondering
Whether I could follow her ass down the sidewalk
And still call myself
A feminist.

**TREVER HADLEY**

## SOMETHING THAT FEELS LIKE LOVE
### by B.B. QUEEN

Wear that black blazer
when you come
to me sticky
with the sweat
of your efforts
join with me
atop a cake
in our Sunday best
balled up
on my floor
where I'll whisper
sultry sounding words
until you fall
asleep
with just my body
draped over yours
keeping you warm
starving for something
that feels like love

**BECAUSE**
by **NICK JAINA**

if you want to lay with me
because you love me
because I am a rainshadow
because I shield

if you want to know my sister's boyfriends
if you want to know my fourth favorite animal

if you want every crumb
if you want to soak rags
and drape them on my fever

if you want my femaleness
if you want the spark of opposition
if you want to color in the block letters

on
every
brochure

it's because you drape your rags
because you shield from love
because of your fever

because the spark
because the block letters

because your sister
because your animal

if you want to
if you want to

because
because

## STEADY
by **KAR JOHNSON**

I don't want to drive fast.

This is a city of shape not speed. I like the way you drive me, guide me through the curves. Fluid almost, flowing imagine. Drunk, grin in the eye and rose cheeked, looking at you as you look at the road, the car loud with laughter. Or. Drunk, rolling down the window and laughing to myself low in my throat, smoking if I can handle it, eyes always shut, guessing where I am by the way we round a corner. Your fingers lace in mine either way. I imagine us like a zipper, our teeth falling into place one after another, how it keeps us together. Without it I'd float out and away. Not sure if you're my anchor or if I'm your weight.

You don't need to drive fast to give me that. Steadiness is reckless too. I know. Didn't think I was scared of going one speed. Maybe it was the illusion of pace. You told me, if you take Great Highway at 35 miles an hour you will hit every green light. It's not fast but it's fast enough. I believed you but not that we could do it. Come up on a red light and you don't stop. It turns just in time. The next one I'm sure we'll need to brake, I tell you. You press the gas, stare me right in the eye, never falter. I get scared, tighten up, exhilarated. We made it. Of course. *Do it again.* I feel the acceleration in my body before you touch the pedal. There are wings coming off of you.

An open highway. Push you through the light. *Do it again.* Make you keep pace, step over the line. But it's you, all you. Keeping us taut like a pulled back bow, and I imagine my spine lengthening at your touch, your other hand a shadow on mine to straighten the arrow, the energy between our bodies conductive, alight as you lean down to my ear, exhale a heat that gives me chills telling me to *hold, hold* until I can follow through.

It's the steadiness that gets me off. The slow come and call. I always think I know too much, afraid there is no way to cheat death so I ought not try. It is soothing to be brought back down by something, not inclined to lean too far out the window, not even think about it. Maybe, though, this is the way we get to love fast, in a holding pattern, not touching down or staying in one place. Steady.

**SHELBIE DIMOND**

## CALIFORNIA GHOSTS
by **EMILY PINKERTON**

The locals are always the same—
blond-haired boys, experts in coy grins,
sweet smiles just for show.
Teeth like yawning nightmares
more Omaha than Oakland
gleam blankly in front of me. Let's dance.
I trace the crescent moon inked on your skin
under the cuff of your rolled-up shirtsleeve. Later
the scars where your skin used to be. (White on the chest,
wine-red on the ankles.) Resistance and pull,
find where the muscle gives. I know you know
your way around oblivion, hold hard enough to hurt.
Turn the lights inside out: let's see whose void yawns deeper.
Let's dance. Starvation wants an end
in emptiness. Give me the click of your marbled teeth
And the ink-drawn snake on the wall. You reach for me
in sleep, pull my arm across your chest.
Rest it over your beating heart
as though a body could ever be sufficient
protection          for something so vulnerable.

## IMAGINARY FRIEND
by **CHRIS MANCARI**

I have a friend, with a body that fits mine.
I have an imaginary lover, made of flesh and bone.
We do not complete, we reflect.
Our sex is masturbation. To lay with him is
as comfortable as laying alone.
I have a friend that I wear like a worn out jacket, it
conforms to my body like a hug, threadbare
it cannot keep me warm.
I have an imaginary lover, made of rage and fear.
Sometimes he is red, sometimes he is blue.
Sometimes there is so much light in his eyes they
blind me, sometimes there is so much dark
they are mouths, they devour.
We love one another like you love your broken self,
disappointed and burdened.
In a clawfoot tub with him on my chest,
he sunk into me, to commiserate. The water gets cold,
the high wears off, the alcohol subsides,
life gets long. I have a friend, an imaginary lover,
that has begun to look like a ghost.

**JACKIE HANCOCK**

## APPLEFORD
by **EMILY PINKERTON**

Give me a brazen woman. Someone who knows how to
shift the engine high, on the whinnying edge of the red line,
tight in the turns. Show me a meeting of eyes, unclouded by
idealization or fear. A kindred spirit. Someone who knows the
difference between fortitude and a jagged edge.

Show me the bite of wind on the midriff, exposed by a too-thin
sweater. Show me forty-one degrees Fahrenheit, pretending to
be on the edge of warmth. Show me grit teeth softening. Lay
the guns down at the perimeter and walk along the fence at the
water's verge. Come inside.

Show me a tightrope balance on a stone bannister, above a
frozen lake, because you can. Show me the rejoinder to the
outstretched hand.

**TAR WIFE**
by **EMILY PINKERTON**

A cloud of smoke and unraveling.
Flimsy feet, shrinking, afraid to stand
next to a man like a wax sculpture. Bright light dimmed:
Small tragedy, all rage and last night's makeup,
bedhead and sweat. Not even sorry.
Not for the stink of stale sex
or anything else. I thought I told you.
Pain swallowed eventually leaves the body
one way or another. Here we are.
I rise, get dressed and nurse,
day after ruptured day.

## YOUR MOUTH
by **JOSEY ROSE DUNCAN**

Use your inside voice. Use common sense. Use your head. Use your brain. Use your words. Use your tongue. Use your eyes. Use your legs. Use your arms. Cross your arms. Close your eyes. Cross your legs. Cross your ankle over your other ankle until the tiny, silver buckle of your 6-inch heel brands your skin where it's taut, where it's paper. Cross your thighs until they're salt, until they're wet, until they stick, until they rip when you uncross them. Speak up. Speak louder. Say something. Why didn't you call. Why didn't you scream. Why didn't you tell anyone. Why didn't you tell me. Why didn't you cross your arms. To hold the beat in, hold your breath. Why didn't you hold your breath. Why didn't you cross yourself. Why don't you pray. Why didn't you beg. Why didn't you drop heavy to cheap carpet, bruising kneecaps, and beg. Why didn't you use your elbows. Your blushing elbows. Why didn't you use your hands. To push. Scratchy, hairy chests. Hot and fleshy chests. Tattooed chests. Smooth, broad tan ones like alien galaxies with 17 orbiting crescent moons. Why didn't you use your palms. Why didn't you use your fists. Why didn't you use your fingers. Why didn't you scratch with your shiny, lacquered, stiletto nails. Why didn't you bite your bottom lip with your incisor till it trembled. Why didn't you shake till wet penny taste flooded your mouth. Why didn't you use your tongue. To lick your lips. To scream. Until your vocal chords turned wool. Why didn't you use your throat. Why didn't you spit. Why don't you remember. Why don't you write it down in your diary with a purple-glitter gel pen. And rip the page where you wrote it from the spine of your diary. Why don't you hold the page to the flame of a white lighter with its safety torn off. And watch your words darken, metamorphosis. Butterfly over sharp rocks that break silty water. Watch your words float over bleached empties and dusty creek banks mapped with boot prints. Fly, burning, into the sun. Why didn't you walk out. In the rumbled hush of 4 a.m., holding your shoes in your left hand. Why didn't you run down the dark street, bare feet collecting glass, asphalt-stained, your pupils wide, flash-bulb, in the buzzed-orange, as soon as you heard the latch click behind you. Why didn't you just leave. Why didn't you just scream. Why didn't you say anything. Why didn't you use your mouth.

## FUCK YOU PART 2
by **RISS ROSADO**

Fuck the lower back pain I got
Bending over backwards for you.

Fuck your Oedipal complex
Your mom is out of her fucking mind.

Fuck whatever she did
I'm not her.

Fuck every night you were too stressed out about work
To get it up.

Fuck you for not leaving work at work
And thinking about it during sex.

Fuck you for making pillow talk about work
Too.

Fuck you for saying you felt like you were about to cheat on me
Go ahead. Fuck you.

Fuck you for saying I'd look great
If I worked out more.

Fuck you for saying you knew you
Couldn't trust a bi girl.

Fuck you for moving to Oakland
After I moved to Oakland
And never answering me.

Fuck every piece I ever wrote because of or in spite of you
Including this: Fuck this poem!

Fuck every time I let you flake with no notice
Playing it super cool to your cold shoulder.

Fuck every orgasm I let you give me
Don't flatter yourself: I've been making myself come since I was 10.

Fuck you for making me be the bigger person
Every time you disrespected me.

Fuck you for making me feel
Twice my age.

Fuck you for letting me down
Then worming your way back into my good graces
And letting me down.

Fuck you for fucking me over
And over and over and over again.

Fuck your radio silence
It's 2018—send a goddamn text.

Fuck the breadcrumbs you left
Leading me back to you.

Fuck you for leaving 9 months of graphic messages to her on your phone
And not having the balls to break up with me.

Fuck you for holding me hostage
And calling it "love."

Fuck you for projecting
I project too but goddamnit
At least I was honest about my limitations.
Speaking of which:

Fuck you for promising to let me peg you
And then annoying me so much I had to cut you off
Before we had the chance.

Most of all:

Fuck you for not knowing yourself enough
To love yourself enough
To even remotely love me.

Fuck you.

## MR. ONE WEEK LOVE
by **CASSANDRA DALLETT**

Though it's fading away
I remember your skin on mine
like a dream like a drug the details already
blurry there was time spent undercover
scratching each other's itches
and busting each other's bumps
or maybe I did all that for you
like the trays of food
I remember
the first date 'cause it came after seven days of sex
each day its synchronicity hard to comprehend
and then on the ninth you fucked it up
and then on the fourteenth you dug your grave

Then I said no and I kept on saying it
I searched for emoticons of middle fingers
two of them wagging at you all the fucks
all the fuck yous
You said if we'd met when we were younger
we would have made ten kids with all our fucking
Alone in my car I scream at you
as if you'll feel me from 89 flat hot miles away
as if you'll come
what I need to scream is no to all of this
no to a man who feels like heroin who feels like crack
who walks out the door with false promises of coming back
When my rage eventually wears off
and the choice comes down
to never seeing you again
or accepting
that you'll dog me out
leave me hanging
on a leash
hungry and desperate for a walk
I know that you know
I will answer the call.

## SOME SUMMER NIGHTS
### by CASSANDRA DALLETT

The brain loops
waiting for his call
if he doesn't love me
no one will
The loop skins me
of looks and pride
leaves hate turned in like an animal's slaughter
like the sound baby goats make when their horns are burned off

The dog terrified of fireworks shivers against me
scraping under the bed
all pant and panic
I drag him out
screaming whiskey breath
The only thing more pitiful than you, dog,
is me and I hate you
Can't bear to look at him wall-eyed and shaking
I push his resistant eighty-six pounds out the door
like I once did a drunk lover
Their need overwhelms, interferes my bath in misery
My longing to be cradled in arms
safe from the booming M-80s and pistols
the flashing police trucks outside
and my heart
exploding.

## THE SUDDENLY SINGLE LIGHTNING BUG DRINKS TOO MUCH ON A DATE
by **CHRISTINE NO**

Why are you sparkling/ at me like/ that?/ I have nothing but this
empty/body-thing/ before you/ just before I/ emptied/       lost
the rest/ my heart/ a boy       /a field,       and fled/ who are you?
/ You are funny / Yes , / I glow/ Violence can be handsome too /a
type/ conflated with humor, often/ don't you find? / I hate/ that
I don't know/how to tell/ different been/ half-a-whole/ so long /
(we mate for life / you know)/ I am prone to giving/ in to bouts
of crippling loss / I've been told       _"hobbies!"_/ I bet / I can what-
if you to death / he called me pet/names only /when annoyed/
_my dear_ / I do much to avoid scenes/ I don't care about win-or-
lose/but / I do enjoy dancing! /yes, the discourse/this dinner is
lovely!/ I _promise! I'm not yelling!_ /just  _excitable!_ / De-escalation!/
is /a handy trait/ but, then, how/ could you say?/ I love you/ the
past/forget  my goodness/       he's gone/ my dear/ I fuck with
intuition / please /don't fuck/ with me/then       aren't you tired?/ I
am/too not a hypocrite / I glow/I don't want to/let anyone / down
/again / I believed/ Magic/ how stupid/ but I didn't/ care / your
awkward/ glower/ just left/ of stage / light trail &/sometimes I feel
seen / shy, too / how cinematic we were / I don't mean/ to swoon/
we're young/ not even Romantic/ just saying/ Okay, I'll keep it/
light/ _HA-HA_ / Oh Riot, / in a small / room /you are not /alone
tonight / What a quiet scene you make/ unavoidably sad/ braver
of two/ hard baring glow /       for whom?/ And yet/ you do/ just
in case?/ that is so       kind/ why does kindness give such pause?

/ Someone called/ me kind, once / and I ran, / confused / what else does one do? / I don't / know how to be my/self/ with/out help/ Oh this body / this faulty / enabled / thing I cling to/ Once I sparkled!/ I glow / light up, / I *still!* /from/time to time/ But/ I was a fire/then, a spectacle/ *Promise! Swear/* I remember: *one time/* glowing bright/luminous prison/ a lovesong-bird / gave me/away/ I had to / I saw him/ emptied/ cupped palm/ screaming/ that wet-lung/skin-boy/ *GREEN! / I know./* I know! */ he loved me!/ And, your excuse? /* So, still do— / night falls again/I glow / *Dear God* I glow / how much can I pretty/enough? / please-oh / *please look!/ His palms are a prison! / please make him* / let *my poor— dear / sweet, Firefly*        go—.

**LUCILLE LARES-KIWAN**

**POSSIBLE**
by **JIAJING LIU**

If
it is
possible
to live in the
in-between-hours, the
minutes when the light must
stay on because otherwise
you can't see through the darkness.
If
it is
possible
to live only
by the glow of
electric lamps, then
it is possible not to miss
the sun, not to think of pansies
as flowers with painted faces, instead
just bits of dried cells stuck between clear panes
of glass, neatly stacked away, with frames attached.
If
it is
possible
to remain in
the same sitting
position, to twist your
legs around, to keep your fingers
moving, then it is possible
not to think about possibilities.

## SUNFLOWER SEEDS
by **KELSEY KUNDERA**

I drizzled my hands in maple syrup
and dipped them in sunflower seeds
to coat my fingers with small crunchy scales.

I walked toward you with a limp,
my left leg forced to carry the weight
of this *thing* in my chest
that is supposed to be in love.

I limped towards you
hands outstretched
dripping syrup and seeds
to show you I could be
both salty and sweet
like you seem to need.

I limped towards you but your face looked appalled.
Disgusted. Disgusted with this food on my hands
that I had put there for you.
Disgusted that I had listened to you
and thought this is what you meant.

I am disgusted too,
but I don't know what to do anymore.

It would be a lot easier if the sex weren't so damn good,
but I should probably look for a lover
who will take my sticky hands and put each finger in his mouth.

Slowly suck off all this syrup I made for you.
Slowly chew each seed I laid for you.
And then keep sucking
even after it's all gone.
A lover who will nibble on my fingernail
to see if there is anything good under there, too.

A man who will look up at me and say,
"Mmmm...yes. I was so hungry."

**CONSUME**
by **PHILIP HARRIS**

Last night, he said, "I wish you could eat me.
I think you could handle it."
I grabbed his thigh and said, "This would be nice and juicy."
He thanks me for being sweet to him.
Sometimes he bursts with laughter.
He grabs my hand during Uber rides.
I want him holding on to me all the time.
I like when my left arm is his.
When we naturally kiss.
When I feel him fall asleep in my arms.
When he giggles because I won't let him leave my bed.
When his face softens in my hands.

**NAKED FOR NO REASON**
by **ALLYSON DARLING**

this is what it feels like
to be naked for no reason
other than that
our bodies fit together
and we both have
flesh
and are not reptiles

we both have hearts
and hurts
and hornyness
that rule us to reproduce
but that we will take every motion to escape
because we don't know each other's last names

shoes that stick
a couch that shakes
strands of hair
wrapped around fingers
long and they get stuck
pulling harder
stacks of slaps
on the chair with the missing footrest
and a complete disregard for
gelled hair
and glasses that get crunched
bent under our weight
yours and mine together
all at once harsh
and more than certain

red cheeks on the balcony
cigarettes in our underwear
we'll wear party hats, too
this feels like forgetting Him

## HAIKUS
by **AMOS WHITE**

she blew his mind out
in a poem slick with cars
—rolling down The Haight


pluviophile—
the way it drips
off your lips


moistened rainbows glow—
your breath ceases to be heard
as the peacock calls

## FAITH
by **JOSEY ROSE DUNCAN**

*For Chelsea*

I build a monument to you every morning
from petals and rose quartz
from sequins and neon
your songs
my bruised pulse
with paper hands

I found a single bud of dry weed wrapped in a white, wrinkled cocktail
napkin tucked into the zipper pocket of your gold purse

I planted it under silt still wet from creek water, still smelling of rot, still blinking
Recited your lost numbers over the seed like a plea

You live on my left thigh
You are made of disco balls
You are made of gerbera daisies
the red ones you tucked behind your ear

You are made of roller skates
You are made of cashew cheese
You are made of mimosas

You are the hot coiled dawn after the party, our caked-glitter eyes never
adjusting to day

You are the bell sound of my name in your throat

You are the bacteria to my gutless marine worm
The lungs we both breathe with
The bullet lodged in my brain

**LUCILLE LARES-KIWAN**

## LADY CUNNINGHAM, ON TWO NIGHTS
### by **MIAH JEFFRA**

1.     grins direct between wreaths of
   twilling smoke, knees keep
   4/4 time with soprano eyes, clarified
   wet, cheeks, and the legs on them,
   oh, how they run. Arms cross
   at the wrists on her lap, elbows
   lean on the woman edge of her.
   Smoke, then fire, then molt, brass
   hair, rivulets down her back.


2.     lifts
   lips and nostrils
   gag rage and run snot,
   fists pound the wall in rapid beat to
   her hoarse deep *fuck*, mouth in loop as
   face bleeds under her pale. Crusted skin and heat
   crack the corners of her mouth. Kneels over my bed,
   Fire, then molt, then prepare for the cooling, her cast of
   brass hair, twisted, hard as rosary beads.

**ANIMAL**
by **LORIA MENDOZA**

He said,
You're an animal in bed.
I was thinking the same thing.
You're an animal in bed.
Like an impotent horse
with a bird appetite,
afraid of a little snail trail.
A misogynist hippopotamus.

## VALENTINE REPRISE
by **CHRISTINE NO**

Delta in-between
My thighs are two continents
Grip them and lay claim

While time stops and starts
Bodies entangled and bare
We are hurricane

Gut me burgundy
Aubergine not rose; bruise, welt
Blood-thick and heavy

Slice down the middle
I am the most vehement
I am slow velvet

Reach inside the maw
Feast if you are not afraid
Of the bite back. Feast.

HANNAH BURGOS

## ABOUT RED LIGHT LIT PRESS

Red Light Lit is devoted to writers, artists, and musicians who explore love, relationships, sexuality, and gender. Since our founding in 2013, we have published 10 literary journals, produced over 50 live shows (including in Austin, Chicago, Los Angeles, Portland, San Francisco, and Seattle), and created a podcast. *Love Is the Drug & Other Dark Poems* is Red Light Lit's first book of poetry.

www.redlightlit.com
@redlightlit